Sabal Palm

Selected Writings
By
Jim McGinnis

Sabal Palm *is a compilation of poetry —*
reflections, musings, and stories from the ragged
but ever-growing collection of this old Floridian.
Fair Winds. -JM

For my family and friends

Sabal Palm
Selected Writings
Copyright 2023. By Jim McGinnis
All rights reserved.
ISBN 9798374744552

He made the long walk home at daylight, a dim and
misty morning with the
Atlantic palpable in the air.
-Jim Harrison

Contents

While Driving

Everything is moving
But the air is still—
The morning is playing for keeps.
My mind is a welter, my thoughts are in heaps.
"Be where you're at," said a girl from the past
From the city that never sleeps.

Be where you're at?
"Pay attention," says Brown Dog,
Letting out a guttural sigh.
"Notice," said Alice, as she went walking by.
Grandpa knelt down in my memory
And kissed a dying bird goodbye.
Harrison sat in a chair by the window
The light changes and I drive on,
A pickup truck cuts through lanes
Covered with slogans of rage.
Ten over the limit, a moveable rant
An old man half my age.

"Behold!" My Shepherd said,
Raising then turning her head.
"There on the wind is a scent."
"Notice," says the Maker,
"Or I'll raise your rent—"
"Be where you're at!"
And I'm still not quite sure what that meant.

And followed the moon through the sky.

Until I see the sunrise.
Glorious oranges and reds begin
To spread across the Eastern skies
And I pull on to the shoulder
To wipe salty tears from my eyes.

Then I continue
Making my run north up Route 1.
And the water now captures my gaze —
The river of glass is all painted haint
And the clouded horizon's ablaze.

That's the way it is with me, you know.
Sober, drunk. shallow, deep —
Miles to go before I sleep.
A part of me, like the moon, is dark
And like my country,
I can get reckless and blind.

The highway is narrow
And though my wheel is true
Still, I weave over the line.
In the fog and haze of days,
I get stuck in the beiges and grays
Of the traffic world.
But this morning is clear, ever so clear,
And I find the Sunrise colors my mind.

Be where you're at.

This Backward Motion

"It's a mean piece of water, my friend,"
He sang, with a ragged voice,
Then finished his drink and threw down
Two fives and a ten.
The man on the stool was no greater fool
For quoting Merle Haggard again.

"Time," he whispered, "is a river."
As it's been said so many times before —
"Moving along like the one in the song,
Washing away all that matters."
Then he stood up and walked slowly
Towards the door,
Leaving me there, drowning in the metaphor.

I never really cared for it much,
Largely because it was true.
Flowing over us, as the poet said,
With us, between us, and through.

I sat alone for a while with my thoughts
Like a book on a shelf,
Then headed down to Sebastian
To work it out myself.
Standing on the southern side,
Watching the boats struggle with the current,
The waves, and the tide.
I tried to think it out alone.
So maybe later, I'd talk it through
With you. And you.
And you in the back on your phone.

This place, this idea
Is in itself a rejection of, a resistance to,
The tide of custom and tradition.
Frost knew though, that the flow
By its nature and its very definition,
Threatens everything.

The glorious forward looking,
Forward moving force
Runs away from our meaning.
Away from our source.

But won't you listen
To what the grandfather spirit is saying
As you toss and turn through your dream:
"The river is calling, *Come up Me*—"
Up against the stream,
Towards memory.

The sheer force of remembering
Is an act of resistance.
Bolstering our defense
Empowering us
To stand against,
To push against the current.

The singer and the song give spirits lift
And yet we wonder why we drift.
But hush now, friends, no need to fret,
Robert Nesta Marley said we can't forget
For the sake of some bright future.
So let the rhythms move us
And do the work of remembering.

 Good Morning, America, I'm your native son.
And America asks,
"Where are you going my darling young one?"
Graceland. Graceland. I'm going to Graceland.
Then back to Muhlenberg County
Where paradise lay.
Back, before the meaning of meaning
Is all but swept away.

What's that you say?
You saw Woody Guthrie's ghost?
You heard slave shouts
Up and down the Georgia coast?

Where are we now?
Where are we headed, blue-eyed son?
Ah, we know the way somehow
By dead reckoning —
From distance and direction already traveled,
From stories and songs already sung.
Voices beckoning
Around turns and bends far flung.

The songs remember. Normandy,
Wounded Knee and the Hundred Slain.
Fleshing out the light and shadows,
The joy and the pain.
Tearing into the guts of a nation.

There are mysteries revealed
In the songs of churches
And porches, factories and fields.
In festivals, carnivals, and smoky bars —
Outcasts and rebels
Brandishing fiddles, banjos, and guitars.
Sing the Blues, Bluegrass, grassroots,
All together.

And we hear Tejano along our trek —
A mix of Mexican, Texan, German, and Czech.
And Zydeco, with sounds of Creole and Creek —
Coushatta, that is…and French Canadian.

What's that you say?
You saw Johnny Cash's ghost?
You heard Pirate shanties
Down the Carolina coast?

The Grandfather spirit is whispering
As you toss and turn
Through your American dream:
"The river calls, *Come up me,*"
Up against the stream.

But what is waiting for us upriver,
Up around the bend?
Some uneasy end?
Along with stories of triumph and joy
And twists of fate,
How bout chronicles of horror
And senseless acts of hate?
The songs remember.
And malice drags us under with its weight,
But giving of ourselves can save us
For love is also great.

Ain't it funny how hard times
Can pull us out of ourselves,
Shedding light upon who and what
We truly are.
Tragedy and trauma
Reveal callouses and scars,
Writing no false memoir.

In connecting hopes and sorrows,
There, the angels of our nature can be found.
Carving lines upon our faces
To run our fingers down —

Reflections in the glass
Now show something deeper, something more.
In our endurance,
We may find other things worth living for
…other things.

In this backward motion,
The traveler cuts the current like a whetted
knife,
Through the unfathomable strangeness of this
life —
Gaining a doglike overstanding, perhaps,
Of an eternity existing before and after us.

Links in the Chain: Haggard/Frost/Parker/Least Heat
Moon/ Marley/Goodman/
Dylan/Simon/Prine/Woody/Cash/Peterson/Jim Harrison

September 21

All dressed up in a fishing shirt,
Corduroys and cowboy boots,
Ready a few minutes early
Before my big commute.

Fifteen to be exact.
I spent them sipping coffee on the hearth
Scratching Stella's back.
You know Stella Grace — a Shepherd
Long and lean and black.

Soon after, I was driving
North up US 1
On the anniversary of my father's death
September 21.

That was a Wednesday
As it is today.
It's been damn near thirty years,
Sometimes I feel like he's still here —
I'm with my sisters by his side.
He never promised to live forever
But I don't figure that he lied,
There was no World Series
The year my old man died.

And for a long time
That number day just hung around me,
Weighing on my shoulders.
Each hurricane season without fail it found me,
Heavier as I grew older.

Sending me on long evening walks,
Bearing the burden of that day
Before the equinox.
Launching me into thoughtful talks
With kids and dogs and ticking clocks.

Time hasn't dulled the images one bit —
My memory of him is as sharp as his wit.
And his tongue.
I hear his voice as I did when I was young,

But there is a lightness, now.
It's changed.
There's something easing the gravity somehow.
It is my age, you say,
The 'something' is earth-born
But I'm not so sure, okay?
A cool breeze passes me
On a hot and humid morn,
Then a whiff of pipe smoke
Drifts by and drifts away —
Giving a loose to this day…
And other days.

Oh, I still have what descendants
Call my Irish moments —
Staring down into the abyss
Of sitting in the dark, listening to Van.
Things happen for a reason such as this,
With no guarantee I'll understand.

I spent a big part of the afternoon
Thinking about it.

Soon after, I was driving
South down US 1,
So long, old lagoon,
Farewell setting sun.

I turned off the radio
Trying to leave the world behind,
Even the weather report was bad
And a decent song I couldn't find.
Just stuck down here in paradise
With the Gulf Stream on my mind.

A storm pounds Puerto Rico
And Hispaniola to their knees.
Say a prayer for old Havana
And my dear friends in the Keys.

But there's a clear sky over Melbourne,
This day is nearly done.
My mood is slowly turning —
My blues are on the run.

Anticipation dances with memory
As I head home on Highway One.
So long, old lagoon,
See you around, old setting sun.
It's my first granddaughter's birthday,
September 21.

Walking the Dog on a Stormy Morning...

With apologies to Robert Frost

Whose beach is this I think I know
His bed is in the condo, though.
He will not see me walking here
With my brown dog and cup of joe.

My canine friend must think it queer
To traipse through garbage far and near
And see the mess we humans make
The grayest morning of the year.
He gives his I.D. tags a shake
To ask if there is some mistake.

Then the sound of loud protest
Of someone out
To make a citizen's arrest.
"No Dogs!" he yells
As we weave our way through irony.

I doubt that he would understand
And so, I yield to his command.
(Resisting the temptation to throw
this bastard in the water)
The ocean's lovely dark and deep
But I have promises to keep…

Seven Times More Slowly

A month ago, or so
I met a Hopi tribesman
On the far side of New Mexico.
He said he saw my spirit fly
There, above the ruins of Chaco Canyon,
Along with ravens and crows
And my Labrador companion.
"But where's my Brown Dog now?" I asked.
"He's waiting for you," was his reply.
"He's waiting — with the others.
Don't ask me how or why."
So, it goes.

In case you haven't noticed,
My mind slips off these days
To places mystical, and there it stays
For long whiles.
In moments transcendent, of late,
Unconnected to illusions of destiny and fate.

Just an old man, with Dogs.
Spirit animals
Lost and found,
Hanging with me, hanging 'round —
Island dogs, Mountain dogs,
And everything in between.
They swim in any water — muddy, brackish,
Blue, or green.
Run joyfully through any weather —
Beats all I've ever seen.
They all love truck rides through town
With the windows down,
And boat rides to the spoils Islands.
Lying by me on the back porch —
Plopping right down
At my feet. On my feet.
Beats all…

Good dogs lost and found,
Yellow, black, or brown,
Tan or gray.
Gone tomorrow, here today,
A mix, three Labs, two Shepherds,
And a runaway.
All thinking that I'm better than I could ever be.
I took a chance on each of them
Each took a chance on me.

Loved ones that I can never keep,
But they come back to me now,
In the fragments of my sleep.

My sadness and my anger bring me tears
As I remember how I whispered in her ear
Just as my last Labrador slipped away.

I reminded her of all the things she loved
And she returns in dreams
And whispers back to me:
"You are no grievous human,
"Get along with all of this that came to be."
"I took a chance on you," she says.
"Thanks for the chance you took on me."
I'll be waiting."

These days, a nervous Shepherd hangs around.
In time, we'll find who rescued who.
Florida Black Wolf — possessing all the features.
And I swear sometimes she casts herself
As that legendary creature —
Wandering the property
As if she's deep down in the Glades
Hunting on her own.
Stalking squirrels and rabbits,
But she leaves the birds alone.

She seems to want to be my friend,
But I wonder if I can go
Through all of that again.
Loving and losing is so damn hard.
I guess that's the beauty of it.
Ah, the Hopi knowledge keeper knows
The truth of loving others, so it goes —
You take a part of each of them
And they take parts of you.
So, there's really nothing else for me to do —
But love.

Seven times more slowly than my dogs I live.
But there must be something left.
Some more of me to give
To my family. To the world.
To this Wolf's descendant
Lying by my side.
She raises up her head
To catch a scent of salty tide
And I say, "I'll get along
With all that's come to be."
I'll take a chance on you, hoping you decide
To take a chance on me.

Sabal Palm Silhouettes

"They're not my favorite," he declared
 Staring westward, showing regret
That the sun would somehow set
Without him —
 "Scraggly, rough and ugly," he said,
Finishing his cigarette.
Who is this, who stopped his walk
Just to get to talk to a man he's never met?

"I'm partial to them," was my reply
As I gazed upon ten sabal silhouettes
Against the early evening sky.

I'm sure he didn't want a tree homily
But all I need is a little shove —
I said, "Their ruggedness in fact,
Is what I truly love."

Saw. Scrub. Cabbage Palm. Sabal Palmetto.
Sabal Palm.
Call them what you will. They won't answer.

You must have seen them
Growing beyond number out in the marsh,
Lining the St. Johns River,
Seeing their reflections in waters mirrorlike.
Bearing scars from wildfires
And lightning strikes,
Their trunks covered by bootjack spikes
That fall away in time.

Hard to kill.
Remarkably indifferent to fires, floods, and cold.
Together, we grew up. Together we grow old.

There, out back, on the edge of salty waters
An old palm lies where it fell.
As a balance beam for my grandsons
And daughters —
Another story I can tell.

Taken down by Hurricane Frances,
Dressed in vines and ferns
It now bears the weight of many dances —
Spins and jumps and turns.

After muttering something about my yard
Resembling Vietnam,
The walker spoke in praise of Christmas palms.
And coconuts, royals,
And other ornamental trees.
I said I loved them too,
Just not as much as these.

I pointed to one out there
Growing crooked and bent
With stubborn, bold insistence.
Upward, then sideways, then upward again.
No path of least resistance,
It meanders and turns
Because of its persistence — its resolve
To keep on going — to keep on growing
After enduring God knows what.

Carolina honors them forever
With a Sabal on its flag.
To our storied past they tend
For lying down together
And saving Moultrie's men.
The Battle of Sullivan's Island,
In the Revolution way back when.
(You oughta read up on that).
"Palmetto State," it is anointed
But is there a Southerner who's disappointed
In the fact these trees know no borders?

My visitor lit another cigarette
And stood, smoking, staring up.
 The evening grew Florida still.
The light faded in the western sky
Robbing me of colors and the will
To preach more to this guy.

He seemed relieved
That I was finally done with talk.
He took his leave and said goodbye,
And resumed his little walk.

But my mood had turned, as it does.
I followed the dog back
Along the old cypress fence line.
And for a while all sorts
Of worries filled my mind.
Thoughts of the future, Troubles of the past,
Then back to the trees, at last.

I could still see shadows and faint outlines
Of oaks and palms all intertwined —
Reminders of my visions as a child
When I'd see them mingling together
In the wild.
My three-quarter acre lot is just a remnant
Of the hammocks and the groves —
What once I saw as treasure troves.

The moon was coming up now
Casting darker silhouettes.
The highway stole my quiet
But I could hear the sound
Of tenor sax and sweet cornet —
A neighbor playing Coltrane over traffic.

And just as quick, my mood turned back.
I guess that's everybody's story:
Contentment is fleeting — transitory.
In depth and height, said Frost,
Happiness makes up for what it lacks in length.
Sounds true enough.
Grace and beauty, though,
Can be often found in strength —
You know, all that stuff — what does not kill us
Makes us…beautiful.

The Sabal Palm taught me that.

We Can Do No Great Things

On some September Sunday
In a pastel dawn, he sat upon the sand
Leafing through his thoughts
On the measure of a man.

Restless member of the human race —
He runs his fingers through his thinning hair
And down the lines upon his face.
Where does he fit? What is his place?
Will he disappear without a trace?
Disregarding Edmund Burke,
He bears the weight of his life's work.

And his faith serves not to comfort him
But to beat and batter.
For within, there lies the burning need to make a
mark; The haunting drive to matter…
And on this fine day,
All good will — all good wishes wash away.

Words reach out from memory — something
Eliot wrote, Of private treasons
One commits for mortal needs —
Doing rightful deeds
For the wrong bloody reasons!
He wonders how he can toss this all aside.
Can he find the strength
To throw off self-importance —
To cast off vanity and pride.

Standing now, he opens up his wallet
And there beneath a wrinkled ten,
He finds a faded, folded page.
Creased and crumpled; worn with age —
There, scribed as verse with a fine point pen,
He reads the lines of a saint again.
The words of Mother Teresa:

We can do no great things.
Just small things with great love.

It was a message given by a faithful one
Who saw beneath his thin veneer.
Who hoped somehow that he
Would someday see
What was to her so very clear.

Faith again served not to comfort but disturb
And bring the man a tear.
For therein lies the mystery
And in the mystery rests the beauty and the fear.

We can do no great things.
We can do no great things.
Just small things with great love.

And this — this was perhaps
A push: a shove, as hopes abound —
From God above; from God within.
From God right here and all around.

Small Revolutions

The threatening storm has cooled things.
We're driving around
With the windows down —
There's a Squall line stretching
Across this town,
The three of us in my old Ford,
Not quite sure what we're heading toward.
There, in the front seat, she and I,
Labrador between us,
Looking worried for the sky.

Rosary in my pocket,
Shamrock hanging from my neck,
Heart on my sleeve.
There's a credible threat of a crash or a wreck
Into something I believe.
Mardi Gras beads swaying on the mirror,
Hula Girl dancing on the dash.
Black dog barking at the lightning flash.

She brushes her hair behind her ear
And calms that old dog's thunder fear.
"No worries, Cicero, it's just the way
That Florida goes,"
Says the girl with the yellow rose
Tattooed across her shoulder.

Should have been a farmer, I muttered,
Feeling rather disabused.
"I remember that movie," she said.
"Shoulda been a farmer, Red."
The woman with the wispy hair sat amused.

In the remnants of the summer afternoon,
We turned off A1A
And crossed the gray lagoon
On the Ernest Kouwen-Hoven Causeway.

She was quiet for a while,
Having nothing much to say.
Soon, she started messing with the radio dial,
Searching for something…
Her footprints on the windshield
Made me smile.

"Didn't Jefferson want us all to be farmers?"
She asked.
"Yeah," I said, nodding.

Declaring my independence,
I crawled across the bridge
With native disdain
For traffic.
She sang along with Creedence —
Have you seen the rain?
Who will stop it?

"Where'd he get that farmer stuff, Homer?"
Cicero.
"Oh, Cicero."
It may have been Horatio
"Well that changes things…"

I shrugged and said
He said a farmer is a free and learned man.
That it ain't just about the plow,
You understand —

"Wide open spaces," she sang…
"Room to make the big mistakes."
"Yeah, that's how it goes."

 Then she glanced back over towards me
And said, "there's a guy right on your ass,"
"And I'm not sure
Why we're hanging out over here
In the left-hand lane…"

I laughed sadly and moved over.
My bitter sense of right of way
Was all in vain.
So much for small revolutions.

"So, what's going on with you?"
With me?
"I know there's something on your mind."
I shrugged and weaved back across
The center line.

Well, aside from the weight of our ancestors' deeds
And the fate of our descendants,
The things I've done and failed to do —
Waiting for my penance? Not much.

"You are so Catholic," she said, reaching over
and gently slapping me upside the head.
I said, *I can't seem to lose these American Blues.*
"Turn here," she said, pointing.
I made a left and then a right
On to Melbourne Avenue,
Mellencamp sang *Little Pink Houses*
As we chugged along behind a bus.
More lightning to the west reminded us
Of what was coming.
Again, the dog stirred.

When the song was over, she spoke again.
"I read once depression
Comes from living too high in the mind."
"Up there, there is no exit we can find"
I didn't say I was depressed. I said I had the blues.

But she kept on.
"Like a dragonfly caught in our garage,
In desperation, he flies around.
And he can't begin to know

A sure way out is down."

That was Harrison, wasn't it?

"Maybe, except for the dragonfly part,
That was me."

"I do love this truck," she said,
Patting on the vinyl seat,
Then hugging Cicero hard.
We rounded the turn toward home
And pulled up in the yard.

The dog jumped out
And she walked right through the house
To the porch,
Only stopping to pour herself
A glass of tea.

And there she sat,
Staring out at the witness tree
With the motorcycle tire swing
That I had painted green, like I do,
She says, most everything.

I sat down inside with Black Dog,
And from the living room
I could hear Tom Petty sing…
First *Breakdown*, then the *Refugee* thing.

And yes, we made our way out,
And she turned to me and asked,
"Who ain't a refugee?"
…we all gotta fight to be free."
I said again, *yeah.*

"That's what it all comes down to."
"Hitchens in the Kitchen, babe —
Petty on the porch."

What was that?
"Come on now,"
"We need to read and listen"
"To all that heaven will allow."
Move our feet when we dance,
And take the bloody chance
To think for ourselves, somehow.

I said, *They didn't teach you that*
In Texas Public schools.

"Oh, I don't know, we Austin kids
Can lead or follow,
Or even be the greater fools."

"Freedom," she said, "is as fragile
As a dozen fresh eggs."
Then turned and caught me staring
At her legs.
And she laughed at me.

"Oh, my Prince of Castaways,
Where is your heart these crazy days?"
"I know where your mind is."

Hey, I'm down, but I'm not dead.

 She laughed again and kept on preaching —
Of taking a knee and making a stand —
Of healing scars upon the land.
About reframing history
And a bunch of other righteous stuff.

I said, *They buried all the dead*
In Robert Lee's front yard, I reckon that's enough.

Not sure I follow…

Stay with me, then
Stay with you?

Oh, bless your democratic wish, I said,
But I think we're lost between our lust for freedom
And the longing to be led —
Caught Somewhere between
Our yearning and our dread.
Oh, this place —
We never seem to know
Who's to blame and who's to bless —
But her infidelities and flaws
Can't make us love her less.
Still, I can't shake 'em,
I can't seem to lose these American blues.

"So…?

So, of all our country's stories — sins and glories —
We only tell in remnants.
That flag won't fly.
I lament the past we've forgotten
With a vengeance.
For with it, goes the promise,
The best of all creeds —
A vow we're bound to break---a zero sum of deeds.

Karma, then?

Karma?

"In the purest sense," she tried to explain,
Standing by the door.
"Is forgetting equal to
The burden of remembering?"
"Who knows what destiny has in store."
"But maybe,"
"The weight we bear
Doesn't make us different.
It just might make us something more."

The creed is worth remembering, I answered,
Even if we can't live up to it.

"Babe, wanna kill the blues?"
"How about we do
Without the breaking news, for starters?"
I said, *Okay.*
"Maybe today's a day we stay away"
"From the phone and that TV" —
"Just you and Cicero and me…sorta."

Sounds like Prine.

She smiled and sang my single favorite line
From "Dear Abby,
And we laughed in spite of ourselves.
**"You are what you are
And you ain't what you ain't."**
Then she stared up at the ceiling
That I had painted haint
To keep the angry ghosts away.

The sky lightened and my mood took a turn
And she walked outside
To check the orchids and staghorn ferns.
It seems the storm blew over —
That's something each Floridian learns
No matter how they got here.
You never know when hope returns.

"I'm late,"
She said
To me without turning —
Late?
"I'm late, dumbass."
"Remember Crescent Beach?"

"I smiled and stared
And listened through the screen…
Thinking about St. Augustine
And our trip to the Ancient City
In the spring.
But the girl who wouldn't wear my ring

Left me hanging,
Hanging on to that last thing.

"Hey,
Why do we have two statues of St. Francis?"
She asked, standing there beneath the oaks.

Well, that one the neighbors gave us,
And the other was my folks'.

She nodded.

I walked outside and stood beside her.
The dog wandered off.
She smiled and leaned into me.
"Stay with me, indeed."

 "We'll be here, with you, and your blues,"
 She said, rubbing her belly.
"Through whichever hurricane,"
"Gust of wind or band of rain."

And she spoke no more
Of dragonflies or refugees.
Just sipped her cold green tea
And watched that tire swing
Move gently in the breeze.
Tom sang "Here Comes My Girl. "

Liam's Toast

I was perched upon my barstool
Intent on getting overserved,
Listening to a woman's rants
Right next to me
On hardship undeserved.
The band was starting soon
And I was hoping for a chance to lose myself
On this stormy Saturday afternoon.

From his place
Way over on the other side,
The Irishman replied,
"Suffering is redemptive."

"No," she snapped.
"Unearned suffering is redemptive.
She spoke as if it were the gospel truth —
A flat fact.
After several minutes, Liam answered back:

"I beg to differ.
No suffering is unearned,
And our troubles are liberating, still —
Survival lessons learned.
Spiritually humbling if you will."
 The voice of St. Francis beckoned,
Along with that of my mother
And John Paul the Second.

The village pub grew silent
Unexpectedly, as the rain outside
Began to fall,
He raised his pint of Guinness
 And proposed a toast
Young Dylan would recall:
"No fear, No Envy. No Meanness."

I raised my glass and took a drink,
But I couldn't help but think
Of what she had said earlier
And how she said it.

I thought of how resentment frames our reality.
Once it has us, it seems impossible to escape–
How we spend our days feeling slighted,
Irritated, and all bent out of shape.

We sit and sip our bitter brew,
Declaring, *I work harder,*
Harder than you.
And I give up more!
Simply choosing to ignore, at any rate,
The uneasy twists of fate.
Our voices are weak and nearly gone
And we're just looking for someone
To blame it on.
Clown fascists play upon our anger and distrust.
Fueling our resentment,
Claiming if you don't hate, you rust.
From the Left wing to the Right wing,
Can't you hear us sing
Resentment Songs?
The politics of protest,
From the Angry North and Bitter South
And Wild and Crazy West.
We like our truth only half-undressed.

"Pardon me?" said that woman there beside me.

"I'm sorry," I replied, "I didn't realize I was
talking out loud."

"Yeah, you were."

"So many of us, sir,
Are in fact, overlooked,
Exploited…disrespected."
I said, yes, "But with a sense of justice
And self-pity intersected."

She glanced at her phone
And muttered something
About inherited poverty and inherited wealth.
"Here's to your happiness and health," she said.

I'm betting you woke up leading off third base,
So maybe you should wipe that insightful look
Right off your face."

The conversation stumbled,
But I had gone too far and drank too much
To turn back now…besides,
The band wasn't very good.
So, I said what I had to, I said what I could.

"Perhaps, if we look up and around," I said, "Not
down."
"Up from dirty knees,
Up through the tallest trees.
What did he say? Less fear, less envy,
Less meanness, please?"

Surely, we can find
Those who endure hardship and pain
And seldom seem to mind.
Who tolerate more and don't complain
Nearly as much as I do…

"So many people out there," she replied,
"Work harder and do more for others,
And have so much less."
"Yes, maybe we ought to treat our failures
The way we do success."

"Amen, sister."

"Did you just call me sister?"
She asked with half a smile.

I let it go right on by
As if I didn't hear.
She motioned to the bartender
To cash her out and order me a beer.
I thanked her, but I noticed then,
That old Liam had disappeared.

The rain stopped and day gave in to night.
And I thought about him,
And I told her how I figured he was right–
 No suffering is unearned or undeserved
And I believed our struggles
Could be redemptive.

"All of my crash landings
That I have somehow walked away from,
Offer clarity and understandings — eventually."

 "So, it is Redemption, after all,"
She said over the music. "Like Marley."

"Well, yeah," I answered.
But the mental slavery
In which we're bound —
Beggaring emancipation
Is a false belief that suffering
Is a badge of validation.
We are not raised up by injustice
And discrimination,
Nor are we dignified by it.

"You feel strongly about this."

"I do."

"We are not justified
In our convulsions and insurrections
Just because we didn't like
The results of free elections."

Though passion may have strained,
It must not break our bonds of affection.
                    -A. Lincoln

As the years roll on,
It's growing awfully clear
That if I could only learn to laugh
At the man in the mirror,
I could strengthen my resistance.
If I shelved my self-importance,
As Harrison said.
I could hold on to the sacredness of existence
And maybe function better as a human

She edged closer.

I am only a doctor, carpenter, soldier, preacher.
I'm just an engineer, police officer, nurse, or teacher.
I'm only a congressman, block mason, writer…
…stockbroker, lawyer, clerk or firefighter.

"But there are birches,"
The woman answered after a minute.
"Some folks are birches.
The white trees Frost wrote about,
So low for long, it's hope
They choose to live without.
Rich or poor"
So low for long they never right themselves.

I listened.

"I got scars," she said.

"And I'm not quite sure how I got 'em.
I don't like the feeling
That I'm sinking towards the bottom.
Any further than I've already been."

"Well, maybe this is why,"
I said, waiting till the song was over to reply,
"Marley called it *downpression,*
Pushing us to be the lowest
And the least,
Beyond the dogma —
The infidel and priest."

"But what about the birches?"
She looked at her phone again
And said, "So suffering is some sort of gift?
Where did that come from?"

"Flannery O'Connor…
Or it could have been my mother."

"Your mother?"

"Yeah, I can't begin to tell you
All that she went through.
But the more she suffered,
The stronger her faith became,
And the more my bitterness grew.
I am none too proud to say out loud
My faith became a field unplowed
For forty years."

"Only in my own sickness did I reach,
Did I begin to understand the lesson
She was trying to teach.
So, I guess it is a gift--what it's all about,
But it sure set me adrift.
Even Jesus had his doubts."

So, say what you will
About this world coming unraveled.
Through live or dead reckoning,
We think we know the way
By distances already traveled.
But out there, anything goes,
Everything is up in the air.
So, it's back to Liam, I suppose.
His toast becomes a prayer.
Less fear, less envy,
And a little less meanness, please.

This time, I glanced down at my phone.
"My ride's here."

"Mine, too."

The Nature of a Place

One of my fondest memories of childhood,
Or was it just a dream I had?
Of standing on the front seat
Between my mom and dad
Cruising up 192 —
What we called New Haven Avenue.
Wide open spaces as far as we could see,
New Haven. New refuge. New place to be.

The car was a 1956 two-tone Buick Special,
Apricot and Bittersweet —
A smile broke over my father's face
As neighbors waved
And we rolled down the street
Apricot and Bittersweet.

From Pittsburgh to Florida
Was my family's not so great escape
To a sleepy coastal town halfway down,
Thirty miles south of the Cape.

Living in the middle of a Grapefruit Grove
Not exactly the dream they sought,
But here they were, like it or not.
And from there my dad got up and drove
North to work with Astronauts.
Engineers and Astronauts.

Now who would believe,
Who would think
Alan Shepherd would be there
To hold a wrench and help him fix a sink?
Or was it, Gordon Cooper?

Up and down A-1-A he went
Each and every day
And all along the way
Was a big blue ocean as far as he could see.

I wasn't around for all that,
Just my sisters and my folks.
Mom had taken sick
And they were forced to pack up and leave,
Desperately searching for somewhere —
Somewhere she could breathe
...and this was it.

For a long time
My dad hated it here —
He missed his city and his friends.
My God, the summer seemed to have no end.
The sun blistered his back
And burned his face —
 But it grew on him — and this became his place.
There came a time when you couldn't get him
Out of here.

He made new friends
And his old ones came to visit.
And the sunrise on the road
To the Cape each day
Took him out, out and away
From all his troubles.

Florida boys courted his daughters,
He got used to drinking sulfur water
...and that beer from Auburndale...*Fisher's?*
And Mom started feeling better,
Which made all the difference.
The only difference.

They got out of the grove
And found a house west of town
On the edge of civilization.
And soon after the great migration,
I came along, swinging a bat
And singing a song —
The family was never the same. Ha!

I grew up in those wide-open spaces
On boats and boards and playing fields,
And so many wild and untamed places.
So it goes, comedies and tragedies,
So, the story flows.

My life's companion, standing
There with hands on her hips
In the doorway
Is the granddaughter of a Key West fisherman —
Descending from Cherokee
And immigrants from Norway.
But like me, this is all she's ever known.

My bloodlines are Irish and Pennsylvanian
But both of us are born and bred Floridian.
Here, on the 28th Parallel and 80th Meridian.
(Put that in your GPS)

Here, in this town, we grew up together
Here — in a town whose sister
Is halfway around the world,
Named by a homesick New Zealander
Missing Australia.

Right here, on the eastern side,
I am no Castaway King or Prince of Tides.
Just a man with his bride
Tied to a place that has given up its nature
Only through hard usage.

Saltwater courses through our veins
And for 50 years,
We've braved the wrath of hurricanes.

The sun has blistered *our* backs
And burned *our* faces—
Shelby was right.
Of all the places,
Here, the air and the heat
Can sometimes be the very same thing.
But not always.

Our place?
It is a small white frame house
On Bignonia Street—our first address
Nothing more, nothing less.
A spot to spend our mornings
Singing Beatle songs…
"Love, Love me do."

Dancing with two German Shepherd pups,
Sipping Maxwell House coffee
From our hand-me-down cups.
"Love, Love me do."

The destination for a pirated Christmas tree,
A fireplace to warm us with fine oak logs,
Somewhere safe to bring home
A son and daughter
And introduce them to the dogs.

A space to return to after saying so many
Goodbyes to mothers, fathers,
Grandmothers, friends.

There's enough joy and sadness to go around
In each and every town—
We need spots where such memories
We can choose to save:
A ballfield by the library,
A tree that shades a grandson's grave.

It's a moveable place — a boat
Which carries me alone offshore
Where I can stand upon the bow
Facing Africa, and leave the here and now —
Depart the century somehow.

A stretch of beach just south of here
With a little cooler full of beer,
Barefoot through the sandspurs
I'd walk the narrow scorching trail with her
Just to reach the blue green water.

Oh yeah, we've done some wandering —
Road-trips to the Outer Banks
And Charleston and Savannah
And to our islands just 90 miles above Havana.

Spent many days on a Carolina mountain
Beneath a giant hickory tree,
Then back down
Through Apalach and Cedar Key,
Following our songlines, if you will,
Crossing the peninsula towards home
And Melbourneville.

But what place is this again? Where are we now?
We've lost our grip somehow.
Here on the Atlantic shore —
The sleepy small town
Ain't sleepy anymore.

We two have paid our dues
With rootholds in the sand,
We've had all the growth that we can handle
All the change that we can stand.
But here we are, where we call home
Greeting all the grands.

So many Junes and Julys
Have taken their tolls.
But watching the ocean, the river and the skies
Can salve our souls.

And soon enough,
We're standing on a spoils island
Marveling at the iridescent colors
Of the water and the clouds.
A sight to behold —
That only heaven has allowed.
There, with our crazy, joyful Labradors,
We could ask for nothing better.
We could ask for nothing more.

I make a mental note to call my son
To float the boat again on Saturday.
 Jimmy will sing us down
The Intracoastal Waterway,
Maybe through the Inlet,
Right on out to the Stream.
Running like a Heartbreaker,
Running down a dream.

Back home again,
Sitting in the rocking chair,
I contemplate another trip.
If we can find somewhere
And get the chance,
I bet I can talk my girl into one slow dance.

Maybe to the Keys, St. Pete, or old St. Augustine.
And it dawns on me as I sit and stare
At palms and oaks
Through the back porch screen
We're neither old nor young nor in between.

We are what we are because of where we are
And where we've been...
 Because we surrendered ourselves to a place
And let it take us in.

My granddaughter bursts through the door
And crawls up on my lap,
Followed by my grandson —
Alas, they have found me and my sacred retreat.
"How about I tell you two about a '56 Buick?"

"Apricot and Bittersweet."

Rootholds

Won't you disregard the notion
That I have been so scarred
From enduring the works
Of a certain Irish bard.
But there was seldom something
To sink my teeth into.
I learned much from St. Thomas and St. Francis
And Maya Angelou.
But there's some stuff out there,
Like Kafka, Sartre, and even Camus,
That can lead a man to stare up at the ceiling
And slump down in the pew.

Voltaire made me laugh,
Mother Theresa makes me cry to this day.
I read one line of Calvin
And went on my merry way.
"Love God and sin boldly."

Indeed, my old professors would probably have
me tarred
For openly admitting that I learned more of
truth
Just from sitting around the barbeque
In my brother-in-law's back yard.

From folding chairs and rickety swings
We spoke of the hope
That baseball brings,
And the mystery of music.

Reading Shakespeare by the fire
And Lincoln on the way,
We burned the candle
With Edna St. Vincent Millay,
Talked of Apolitical Jesus
And Jefferson,
James Whitcomb Riley and Stephen V. Benet.

The man taught me things. Things of value,
And never mind the cost
He set me on a course to cut my teeth
On Sandburg, Twain, and Robert Frost.
And sometimes still I like to sit outside
In the remnants of a day
Chewing on the words of Ernest Hemingway.

Sitting at the bar down by the marina,
He had a mind to teach —
"Stay curious, Jimbo," he said.
And something else about my grasp and reach.
"Intelligence and common sense
Are there, I'm sure, for self-defense
And I could use some more of each.
But the prophets speak in present tense."

"Scholars and artists are good company to keep,
Showing us a big old world
Both broad and deep —
A blending of thought and emotion.
For a life is not some pool of water
But a fathomless blue ocean."

"Angels live in Libraries,
But take a look around.
In barbershops, at bus stops,
And exchanges over countertops,
There is a wisdom in the commonplace,
Just waiting to be found."

"From smoky tavern conversations
(Remember those?)
To park bench visitations
With lonely folks downtown — flesh and bone —
Living out their lives,
Finding meaning on their own.
You can't find it all written down,
For the truth ain't always leather bound."
"On the other hand,

If we belittle all that we don't understand,
And rely only on our instincts
And our native wit,
We might just find ourselves embracing
A narrow truth that seems to fit,
Disregarding all else."

"Surely, there will be no happy ending
Living in the matrix or the cave.
Our lives resemble shadows on the wall.
We chase the getting and the spending
As a goal and not a means
Of giving purpose to it all."

There at the bar, in spite of ourselves,
We speak of democratic sin,
Of *Slaughterhouse Five* coming off the shelves,
Along with *Mockingbird* and *Huckleberry Finn*.

My brother, in or out of law,
Always calls it straight, just the way he saw —
"Why on Earth," he asked
With a disbelieving look,
"Would we ever think to burn or ban a book?"

"Gathering knowledge," he declared,
"Is not elevation or emasculation.
It is liberation."

"That's enough, I think I'm going home."

Turn the page, I say.
Oh, please come on by and sit awhile,
We'll talk of things that make us smile.
There's a breeze across the porch today,
I'll open up a couple beers
And put on some vinyl records
We haven't heard in years.
Oh, let the stories flow.
Of Ted Williams and DiMaggio…

Of kids and dogs, of oaks and palms,
And orange moons rising.

I'll recite some lines of poetry
And share with you my secret stash,
You sing to me some songs
Of Kristofferson and Cash.

"Okay, Okay," he answered,
"I'll come by for a bit."
And we talked more of things —
Saturn's rings and tire swings
And the lonely song the highway sings.

The rootholds of a learned man —
Finding meaning on his own, you understand.
On his own but not alone.
And I forget at times,
He's made of flesh and bone.

Reading Shakespeare by the fire,
Reciting lines from *Lonesome Dove*.
Pondering *the Prince Tides*,
And the wonder of falling hopelessly in love.

Scholars and artists are good company to keep,
Showing us a world both broad and deep —
Miles to go before we sleep.

Yellow Bicycle

I woke up early
With music in my head,
From my *Groundhog Day* clock radio
Blaring The Grateful Dead
And something a guy named Chatwin said
In a book I read twenty years ago.

I stepped out of the shower
And over the dog,
Thinking of what the morning had in store.
I think both of us were looking forward
To being on our way,
To our walk along the eastern shore.
But it was memory that carried the day.

It would be light soon.
I made half a pot of coffee,
Got dressed, fed that dog,
And let her walk out back.
I dropped some brown sugar into my cup —
I usually drink it black,
And stirred it with the one clean spoon.
Then we were off, upon our walk,
Beneath the fading stars and crescent moon.

I was humming, whistling, singing to myself —
Four mile an hour pace.
A four-beat rhythm to my step
With a smile upon my face.
The dog stayed out front,
Pausing every once in a while
Letting this old man catch up.
The sky lightened.

That four-beat stuff
Comes from the Bushmen of Australia.
They believe the world was sung into creation.
          (I first learned that
          From Chatwin and Jimmy Buffett).

They claim we follow songlines
And the music leads us on our way.
In the footprints of our ancestry —
To this very day,
We keep searching. Searching for some grace.
But how's the saying go?
In our trek through time and space,
The path is walking too.
Can all of this be true? Who am I to say?
One who named his Labrador a prophet.

My thoughts turned in that direction,
As dawn gave way to day
And I got all caught up in it.
But I was rescued for a while, at least
By a recollection running around my brain —
The image of a girl on a yellow bicycle
Singing softly an old John Prine refrain.
...I'm sorry my son but you're too late in askin'.

When I lived in Gainesville years ago,
I spent a lot of time outside,
Getting away from worldly things,
Playing my Gibson six-string,
Letting all of it slide.
And I remember one evening,
I was out on the porch after the Spring Arts Fest
Drinking cheap red wine, trying my best
Not to butcher a favorite ballad of mine,
When I noticed a girl on a bike
Leaning on the bridge railing, listening.

I don't think she could see me
From where I sat on the step,
But I could see her, holding her hair
Up off of her shoulders
And I had to look twice.
She started singing along
As I got to the chorus of "Paradise."

I stood and smiled sadly at this memory,
Right there on the beach —
The dog stopped and stared back at me,
And a sweet regret returned
From a time so far beyond my reach.
Or was it?
It's a mystery why I didn't walk out
And talk to her,
But I kept on and she was gone
By the time I finished the song.
I never saw her again.

I remember shrugging,
Somehow thinking it was okay.
But later, it hit me.
Had I seen her before that day?
I would have remembered.
I thought again of songlines — hers and mine
And how they may have crossed.
With no idea then or now,
Of the value or the cost.

She just might be remembering bits and pieces
Of this herself, somewhere.
While on a bike ride across another town
Or maybe while holding her grandbaby, there,
In an old hand-me-down rocking chair.
I'd like to think it was her mother's,
Brought down from Apalach or St Augustine,
Freshly painted avocado green.

Perhaps she sang a soft song in that rocker,
Consoling a crying child, helping him endure,
Taking them both back to our beginnings
When movement soothed us
And made us feel secure.

It's a funny thing about music,
It can steer us,
Or at least salve our souls in uncertain moments.
We are stirred by the rhythm, and a gentle beat.

"Did she dance?" I wondered.
"Well," she might say, smiling,
"I like to sway my shoulders,
And shuffle my feet,"
"You gotta move your feet."

If I could, I'd ask her if she read Chatwin's book,
I'd tell her about my own strains
And strands and lines
Weaving through the mangroves,
Stretching down to the Caribbean Sea.
I'd talk about the old piano out on Cabbage Key
And a jukebox in an airy little waterside joint
Just north of Grant called Castaway Point,
A place that doesn't even exist anymore.

And I would listen as she told me
About her own streams and threads.

But she might not say anything at all.
She may only remember
A perfect bike ride
Accompanied by a song, she could recall,
So many times, spilling from her brother's room
Across the hall.
Maybe she remembers only the pond
And the bridge
And her love for Gainesville.

I would probably say too much,
I'd throw it all out there —
Unwilling to lose what I did not know
I had to gain.
I would talk about the links of chain
And the mystical tones,
And hope she remembered Prine's Refrain.
"Won't you sing with me again
On this warm spring day?"
Down by the Green River where paradise lay.

It comes back to the songs, you know.
The Bushmen were right.
In the memories of immigrants,
The dreamings of aborigines,
In the achings of natives,
And the longings of refugees —
The song is the door.
It is music that opens us up —
That reaches to the core.

The jumbled mixture of events
In the songs each singer sings —
Are the cadences and rhythms
That our living brings…
All our joys,
Tempered by the hard times, salted by the tears.
Our hopes and dreams and dreads and fears,
And yeah, the laughter all mixed up
With the rest of it.

So, here, on the other end of a life,
I still sit out on porches with my dog,
Or lean on the hood of my American car
And finger pick three chords
On my ancient guitar,
Keeping my eye out for yellow bicycles.

Still searching for some grace,
Refusing to believe
We disappear without a trace.
Holding on to memories
Like books on my shelves,
Thinking, maybe that along with ancestors
We walk unwittingly
With our once and former selves.

The centerfielder brushes by,
Racing, chasing a long, high fly.
The sunburned Floridian casts a line,
Standing on the bow of his boat.
The young teacher keeps preaching
As the boy's nap deepens.
The old man stops to rest
As the slope of the road home steepens.

And the guy on that porch
Sees the girl on the bike
In a halter top and faded jeans,
There on the rusty bridge railing she leans.
And he starts writing a song,
That he knows can't begin
To say all that it means.

Songs are wise, that way.

Believer

Last time I set my feet on land
It was right around Election Day.
I bought myself a pair of Sunday shoes
And headed in to listen
To the reverend preach the news.
But on the street outside, where hopes abound
I turned and heard
The smoky sound of saxophone.

Then found myself wandering down
To sit on steps with an old Black man
Who tried to make me understand
That God is all around.
"Please play," I say,
"Just play the Blues so we don't have the
blues."

Got to get 'em out, Irishman, he replied.
Out and away.

Then play he did,
With the soul of an ancient
And the heart of a kid,
Beneath that old canvas awning.
But it wasn't just the Blues. It was Coltrane.
Dear Lord, there in the lightly falling rain
Dear Lord.

"How'd you know I was Irish?"
I asked when he finished playing.

He laughed, and pointed to the shamrock
Hanging from my neck.
And that pink skin of yours gave it away.

What have you been doin' on that boat of yours?
He asked.

"Drifting. Drifting out, a mile or two offshore,
That's where I like to be.
The tide pulls, the wind pushes,
The currents flow,
But no man drives me."

"And how'd you know I was a boatman?"
He laughed again.

Why church, then?

"I could use a few prophets," I answered.
"I don't know about you.
Maybe a Christian, Hindu, Muslim or Jew.
I'm thinking maybe a Buddhist will do."

Well, he said, *My own mind is my own church,*
Old Tom Paine would say.
I'm the captain of my search — out and away.
You gotta be your own priest
On this journey down to become the very least.
Out, down, and away.

Where you from?

"Me? Here. Never lived anywhere else
But here."
"Family came from Pittsburgh
After World War Two."
I asked him if by chance
He knew 'The Foggy Dew.'
I do not, he answered without apology.
"Too bad."

So, when did they come from the old country?

"I don't know. 1880?"
Then he laid it on me.

People weren't actually coming here, you know,
They were getting out of —
The hell out of, and away from…there.
All that degradation, oppression and despair.

"Except your people," I said. "They were taken."

My people? He replied without emotion.
Most of my kinfolk were runaways. That's all I know.
Fleeing to the Everglades —
Adopted by the Seminole
And other renegades…
They moved to the islands, away from Crow,
Then back here when I was young,
Forty or Fifty years ago or so.
My folks told me lots of Irish were brought down
To Jamaica…indentured servants…my bloodlines.

I said I didn't know that.

Yeah, that's the way it is all over, he answered.
But here, in this place lives an idea,
Any man or woman,
Free from all the brimstone rants.
Can take their liberty at second glance —
Disenthralled, as Lincoln said —
Free in great wide-open space,
Each can find a sovereign grace.

Then he played some more. This time it was
Wise One, I believe.

I glanced down at his luggage
And wondered if he was some sort
Of traveling preacher,
Or maybe in his heart of hearts,
A history teacher.

He kept playing for a few minutes,
Then muttered something else
About wide open spaces.

Somebody needs to hold on – to remember.
The idea, the dark man said, *is one we can't forget*
Just because we can't live up to it.
It's no load to carry.

"Maybe it is. Maybe it ain't," I replied.

He seemed not to hear me
And spoke again of folks moving,
Out and away.
Out, out and away.
But they were chased across the continent.

"Yeah, chased or run over," I added.

Ha! He went on.
First the smoke of another man's chimney
I guess that's okay
But soon a town all made of blocks
With many doors and many locks.
Then a bank or two, and church with steeple –
To ring the bells, summon all the people.
We sing those hymns and ring the bells.
But beware, my friend,
With priests and dogma come the infidels.

Now, that dogma part was Jefferson…
You know Jefferson? he asked.

"Yeah," I answered.
"I know he was a shadow man,"
"So, I try to take in all the good I can.
The rest, well…"

After all these years, he interrupted,
I guess we've found that we still need him.

Then, what's the purpose?" I asked.
What's with this talk of freedom?
He shrugged his shoulders.

What would the red-haired wonder say?
I bet it would be something
About getting out and away.
It's a gift, you know.
We're obliged, not just allowed
To cut a path uncharted; to live a life unbowed.

"Whew!" I said.
"I think you've been reading my mail."
Then I stood up slowly from the steps,
Holding on to the rusty rail.

The sky lightened and a breeze blew,
Taking with it all the rain.
I was heartened by his lesson.
Strange how truth can keep us sane.
He played then stopped again.

I thanked him for helping ease
My American blues.

Where you going, Irishman,
In those shiny Sunday shoes?

 I looked up at clearing skies,
And then over at his old smiling eyes.
"I might find a ballgame,
Or head over to the library."

He said angels live in libraries.
Last time I went I had to step over one
Sleeping in the doorway.

I smiled then turned and wandered off,
Looking for some Jefferson,
Whitman, or Thoreau —
Maybe some Dylan, I don't know.
I'll take a little time and trouble,
Spend some hope,
On Tuesday, cast my vote,
And then I'll go…
Go to the woods or back on the boat
And try to find Jesus on my own.

A Great Small Flag
Unstuck

There he was, out on the porch
When I pulled up.
CR didn't seem to notice me.
He rocked away the summer morning
With his German Shepherd pup,
Slowly sipping on his tea
With the spoon still in his cup.

"You'll put your eye out," I warned him
But he didn't seem to care.
He just patted the dog and sang a song
To someone who wasn't there:

Jeannie, won't you lay with me
And scratch my back a while,
Whisper in my ear
Sweet things that make me smile

Ever since he quit the booze
He sits out here and reads the news
And worries about his country.
CR flies a little flag on a stick taped
To the lamppost,
A Christmas wreath still graced the door.
Finding nothing to fall back on,
He drops the paper on the floor.

"Sean," he said, "They're taking books
Right off the shelf
And I don't feel so good myself."
Staring out into the sunburned lawn,
He kept on rocking, rocking on, still talking —
"A bobcat killed the rooster
Down at Honest John's."

I wasn't sure of what to say
Or just how I should respond
But I promised I would buy him a flag
Of decent size.
He told me not to bother
And wiped the water from his eyes.

"I figure anybody who can fly a great big flag
Can fly a great small one," he said,
Gazing out towards my pickup truck.

"A little girl gave me that one
At the Veterans Day parade.
She sat down right beside me on the curb
And drank her lemonade.
We spoke of kindness, love, and beauty
In the universe displayed."
Then he sang another song:

Billy Pilgrim, they will burn you,
Just you wait and see.
It seems you've made the list
Of Moms for Liberty.
Guilty of the heinous crime
Of coming all unstuck in time,
Billy, you've been a friend to me.

"Is that you, CR? Coming all unstuck?" I asked.
I recognized the line from a book
He made me read in high school.
"I guess," he answered.

"But Vonnegut was with your Pop
In World War Two.
A nightmare. No big deal, they said —
Just what they had to do.
Billy, he won't work on Maggie's farm,
And he sure won't study war no more."

I leaned on the post and nodded
But I couldn't really comprehend.
And CR sang his verse again.

Then, for the first time, at least with me,
He spoke of Vietnam.
"They drafted you right out of school?" I asked.

"Who told you that?"

"My Mom."

"Yeah, I won the lottery."
"Number 93, Spec 4, 25th Infantry."
He talked about Long Binh and Cu Chi,
LZ's and IED's.
And losing two friends from Indiana.
Sleeping in the rice fields
To hear Charlie coming out,
'Didi Mow!' The GI's shout —
Dinki Dow and getting out of there somehow
Before he turned 21.

"I made six fifty a month.
Sent all but forty of it home
Except for the time I went to Australia."

"You went to Australia?"

"Hell, that was 50 years ago.
Everybody was talking Thailand,
Said Australia was way too far
For just a week on R&R.
I had my heart all set on Sydney, though,
Spent a week there with an older woman there,
Don't you know."
He shook his head and laughed.

I told CR that I once had a science teacher
Who served.
A Helicopter pilot.
He had an eyepatch and a scar
Down the side of his face,
Looked like a pirate.
Talked politics at the drop of a hat—
Called himself a Southern Democrat
I forgot I remembered him.
He was always walking around
Swinging his old baseball bat.

Offered no war stories—
Said he was just glad to be alive.
One of the last to leave Saigon in 1975
Before it fell.

It was quiet for a time—
Neither of us said a thing,
Both of us sweat the sweat that summer brings.
But afraid he couldn't hear the songbirds sing,
CR refused to use the fan I gave him.

He stared out again across the lawn.
He kept on rocking, rocking on—
It seemed to comfort him,
But then he stopped.

"She wore a yellow sundress."

"Who?"

"The little girl with the flag.
Dawn. She said her name was Dawn.
I liked that name.
Last week a shooter walked into her school
And now she's gone."

"What?"

"Along with 20 others, she is gone."

"What am I supposed to do with that?" I asked
after a moment.

"I don't know."

CR raised his index finger
Then got up and walked inside
Without completely straightening up —
The dog followed.
He returned with a ragged journal and some
reading glasses
And read to me Vonnegut:

*Be soft. Do not let the world make you hard. Do not let the
pain make you hate. Don't let the bitterness steal your
sweetness. Take pride that even though the rest of the world
may disagree, you still believe it to be a beautiful place.*

CR closed his journal
And started rocking again.
I was flooded with thoughts
Of children and forgotten old men
And books in America getting banned.
The fact I didn't understand
Stirred me now —
I wanted to cry, but I didn't know how.

So, I stood there, still leaning
Behind my thin disguise
Clouds were building now,
Out in the western skies
And a breeze began to blow.

*Jeannie, won't you lay with me,
Scratch my back awhile.
Whisper in my ear sweet things
That make me smile.*

It's Good to Know

...driving down the lonely road
Forty-seven miles from home
At ten damn thirty on a Thursday night:
As I cross the St. Johns River,
I see a boat offshore —
It's good to know
There are men fishing, tonight.
It's good to know
There are men in taverns,
Perched upon their barstools
Talking politics
And swapping tales of the great Ted Williams.
It's good to know
There are old men sitting in their dens,
Reading —
Dozing off every now and then...
And there are men telling stories to their kids
Then kissing them good night.
As I blast across Route 50
Headed for the coast,
I think back upon a week of work and worry,
And I curse my maddening hurry.
Still, it's good to know there are men fishing.

Disenthralled

I don't get to Church a lot these days.
So many things that I believed
Have fallen by the ways.
I don't get to Church a lot these days.

It's hard to get your hopes up anymore.
Every time you do
Fear knocks you to the floor.
I don't get my hopes up anymore.

Truth is strewn like dry leaves on the ground.
I can't feel much good will — it seems
That there ain't much of that around.
Every time we stand to speak
We're shouted down.
But I talk to God a lot these days I've found.

She sees Him in everything, she claims.
And admits that there are times
She feels a bit of shame
For trying hard to earn what He gives for free.
Grace can't help but get the best of me.

I can see the light in children's eyes.
Their tears and laughter strip me clean
Of all my alibis.   They take me back
Where faith is raw, and love can disenthrall.
I might get my hopes up after all.

I may not get to Church much anymore,
But I feel closer to my Maker
Than I ever was before.
Spending Sunday mornings
Beneath the shade of ancient trees,
Or walking down the beach
Just to feel the salty breeze
Grace can't help; but knock me to my knees.
PS: I went to Church last Sunday

Down a Mangrove Coast

Well, I'm seldom one to boast
But few have had a morning quite like mine!
I planed across glass water
Down a mangrove coast,
Heading for a place to cast my line.
A solitary trip,
But I brought along the dog
For necessary fellowship
And cordial dialogue.

Just North of Pineda,
A spot familiar to me Marked by six palms
And a gumbo limbo tree.

I never caught much there,
But boy, the dolphin do.
And to speak what's true
On this fine day,
I'd rather watch them anyway.

The boat was hitched and ready —
All done the night before
I just had to get on up and go.
Packing peanut butter crackers
And a thermos full of Joe.
Tackle box, boom box,
And a crazy Labrador.
We beat the dawn by minutes
I could ask for nothing more!

Under the bridge
And through the channel —
The lagoon that I love best.
In a simple, semi-sturdy craft.
An '89 Key West.
Seventeen-footer, crude and coarse,
Powered by an old Johnson 70 horse.
My friend, a boatman by his trade,

Said it's among the finer motors ever made.
But even with that accolade
It's a wonder I'm still running her.

A boy from Mississippi wrote
He coveted his little boat
To tote him in and out of habitation.
And so, it is with me —
My peculiar avocation
Aboard a stripped-down shallow V:
The weatherworn "Plan B."

Not too often the one to boast
But few have had a morning
Quite like mine.
As I planed across glass water
Down a mangrove coast,
I raised my coffee cup toward heaven
To propose a grateful toast.

An Overdue Introduction

I heard a guitar player say once, "It's all about the blues, man…we sing the blues
so, we don't have the blues." But I think some blues are made to stick around, and I don't mind that. This is for my daughter, Meagan and her boy, Tiernan.

Let me introduce myself. I'm your grandfather. I come and sit here at your grave beneath this ancient oak. I am a very blessed human—I'm surrounded by family and friends. My other grands—your sisters and brothers and cousins— bring much joy into my life.
They're often loud and wild and crazy, and they can irritate me sometimes. But I start missing them as soon as they pull out of the driveway. I'm usually a very grateful old dude, except when I'm here beneath your tree, and I think of you and your mother, my daughter. I don't understand anything. My faith is too weak to allow me to be grateful here.
Your mother too, is blessed, both by those she loves beyond measure and those who love her without condition. Even as we celebrate and give thanks for our gifts and good fortune, your grandmother and I still mourn for you and ache for our daughter. It is so hard to speak of, we seldom do.
Normally, I just sit here and stare down at your grave, taking time to brush away any leaves that may have fallen. But today, I feel like I should finally introduce myself. Your grandmother says that I'm grumpy, but I think you would have liked me. Surely, you would have loved her. And this is my dog, Stella. She came with me today. Stella Grace. She was friends with our two Labradors who you would have loved and called your own. They would have licked your face and stolen your cookies. Indie would have

raced you to the bottom of the pool, and Marley, well, he probably would have taken naps with you, as your furry pillow.

Their souls and spirits are elsewhere. Perhaps you know them. I hope you do.

Your mother is brave. So brave. She confronts her sorrow and wears her love for you on her sleeve each day. But your grandfather is not brave. I try to file you away in my heart until the next time I mysteriously find my way to your oak on some beautiful day. But I am unable to choose when you your memory visits — at ball fields and on boat rides and walks along the beach, and out on my back porch.

We don't really know what happens when we lose someone. We say we do, but I'm one human who is unsure. But I do know — I think I know — what love is. Sure, it is the giving of oneself to someone or some thing. but how does it feel? **Love,** I heard a priest say, **is the overflowing effervescence of being**…a bubbling up. It is willful and selfless, yet sometimes, it comes to our hearts without permission. What to do? My friend, Dave, calls it mud. "Jump in the mud of love." I like that.

It takes courage to love. It's easier when you're young to immerse yourself…to open yourself to it. When you're older, you know the stakes — the cost of letting someone in. In your case, it didn't matter. Your love found me anyway.

I saw the tears in your mom's eyes as she held you, and I know it was love overflowing. Grief comes soon after, but not without love, first. Grief hangs around to remind us of the depth of our love. It's worth the pain…the tears.

When I'm standing or kneeling here, I often ask
myself if there is another place, an elsewhere.
What do I believe? Well, I'll tell you what I
don't believe:

As the poet said:
*"I don't believe a heart can be filled to the brim
then vanish like mist.
And that's all there is that ever exists."*
-Paul Simon

I don't think I could have said it better. Love is
proof that our souls and spirits go on,
somewhere. I'm betting somewhere close. That's
all the immortality I could hope for. I'm figuring
love isn't something. It's the only thing. My love
for you guarantees we'll meet again. And I'm
good with that.
And this is why I hear myself saying your name
as I drive down US 1 or A1A. This is why I visit
every once in a while, to brush the leaves away,
and look up through your tree on a beautiful
day at the blue, blue sky.

Songlines

Standing on the dock with both hands
In my pockets
Staring off across the dark lagoon.
Celebrating my thirty-ninth birthday
Waiting for the August moon.

Something of a calling stirs inside of me —
Some voice, some ancient rhythm
That urges us to flee
The comfort of the village
For a journey on the sea.

There's a songline
Weaving through the mangroves
From an old piano out on Cabbage Key.
With words of validation and redemption
In stories shared by friends and family.
Reaching back to Boston, Massachusetts
Through harmonica
And weatherworn guitar.
There are voices spanning generations
Hardened by the rum and good cigars.

There's a songline
Running through Savannah.
I hear it stretches down to Florida Bay!
Or maybe all the way to old Havana.
We'll find it on some bright September day.

But there's a squall line
That spans the intracoastal.
Lightning flashes cut across the sky.
The blowing rain jabs my skin like needles,
But the echoes of the music hold me by.

Oh, there's an old tune
That plays out on the salt air
From a boom box bungeed to the bow.
Many travels; few destinations,
But the memories that I visit lift me now.

Like a sunset I remember off Shell Island
And a moonrise
I recall on Melbourne Beach.
There are children laughing in the rain
Out in my driveway!
There are moments we're beyond the mortal reach.

There's a songline
Running through Sebastian
From an old piano out on Cabbage Key.
With thoughts of home
Before the Great Migration
In stories shared by friends and family.
Reaching back to Pittsburgh, Pennsylvania
And from Irish pubs
With old men raising jars.
There are voices spanning every ocean
Sweetened by the beer and good cigars.

...sitting on the steps
in front of old St. Joe's
waiting silent for the morning mass.
But on this holy day my mind wandered
Off to narrow channels made of glass.

Jefferson on the Porch

I was sitting on the back porch
Pondering Eliot's treason,
Reading just my second book
Of this, the hurricane season.
Again, it dealt with Jefferson —
And yet another look
At America.

My attention shifted
First, to the brown dog lying at my feet
And then to all my summer chores
That would take me out into the heat.
But then back again to the great Virginian.
Something kept me there in front of the fan
Planted in my seat.

On that humid morning, I read on —
One more lesson he had to teach.
Of his belief in a moral sense
A benevolence slumbering in each.

…Don't need a prophet or a prince, said he,
To tell us right or wrong.
An inner voice — the conscience —
It's been here all along.

But Liberty's apostle owned a slave. (Or several)
(or many)

 How could it be
That he was first to write a law
To set a people free,
But could not bring himself until the end
To emancipate dear Sally?
A hero? You say now,
With the sin that he commits,
He preaches from the pulpit of the hypocrite!
A hero? I say yes. *Because* he's fallen.

Ah, hypocrisy — Our favorite sin.
And Jefferson knew his crime. He saw it plain.
He smelled the stench and felt the pain.
But if in moral contradictions
Lie the measure of a man,
Then who is worth a damn among us?

And I've heard others say it:
From the deep and dark recesses
Of our own self-betrayal,
There — the force of moral vision rises.*

*As the sun crept up in the sky
A gentle breeze began to rustle in the trees,
And the dog is restless now,
Impatient with my sedentary ways.
He probably wonders how
This human could be stuck in such a daze
With all the world before him.
Still, I sat and thought long thoughts...*

If within, there is capacity for good,
Our darkness then, won't be denied.
Man's two natures, rightly understood,
Can't live side by side
But in some constant fight.
I do believe the ancient Greeks
May well have had it right —
Long before Virginia, they tried to understand
The curious forces in the making of a man.
Others said this, too.
Their myths were metaphors of human nature
And the battles that ensue.

The Age's optimism broke with a red sky
And dawn went down to day.
Still, the ghosts of Hobbes and Calvin loom.
How then do we keep our wickedness at bay?

We are violent and corrupt, we are selfish.
We are weak.
Wealth and power, we boldly, blindly seek.
Disorderly, chaotic,
Contentious, and profane.
It's clear enough, we have to be constrained.
But we're joyful and creative,
Filled with verse and song.
We are selfless and forgiving,
Compassionate and strong!
And we must have the right
To find a life worth living —
Free to find our way along.

But of all the philosophical stunts,
How can we be bound and free at once?

Old Locke won't take it quite this far,
Insisting we're inventions of the world…
"Waxen shapes we are!"
Tabula Rasa…created not within, but out.
There seems little room in him for doubt!
And volumes have been written —
Taken down and passed along as fact.
That only on self-interest do we truly act.

Now then, a debt is owed to Locke —
"Newton of the mind"
His books impress my friends,
Sitting there upon my shelf.
But the only motive he can find
Is that which benefits oneself?

Where's the moral sense?
The pleasure gained by helping others?
No need to come to Jefferson's defense.
Like the Scot before him,**
Our beleaguered founder — enlightened pioneer
Believed there is no place for determinism, here.

In Calvin, Locke, or Freud,
Whatever the disguise,
With dogma comes iron fetters.
Try on your own free will for size!
"When I do good, I feel good," Lincoln said
His simple creed rings true.
Man and woman must awaken to
What Jefferson already knew:
There's got to be benevolence
In the happiness we doggedly pursue…
…even if we never catch up with it…

*"Benevolence" — *Gary Wills claimed Jefferson departed
from his contemporaries by insisting that we are born with
* a moral instinct; believing it to be the basis*
for all politics and morality.

Francis Hutcheson *was one of the founding fathers of the*
Scottish Enlightenment.
Inventing America. *By Gary Wills*

The American Soul. *By Jacob Needleman*

Gratitude

picking up a Conroy quote and running with it.

Because of you-- my English Teachers, friends
and mentors--I found tongues in trees, books in
running brooks, and truth in poems, songs, and
movies.
I got "tangled up in blue" and I felt "Sunday
Morning coming down." I sat at the window all
night and watched the moon until it set just
before dawn. I skidded down a Mangrove Coast
with Louis, L' Amour, and got away from Earth
awhile, atop "Birches" in New England.

I noticed the color purple in a field, and I saw it
in the waters of the Gulf Stream.
I stood at Gettysburg. And with a debt to
Flannery O'Connor, I took a journey through
sickness, a place where nobody can follow. I
visited the ghosts of my father's heroes in Iowa,
or was it heaven?

I've been to Paris looking for answers and down
to Captain Tony's to get out of the heat. I was
there with Augustus McRae sitting around the
campfire, reading Leviticus waiting for the
biscuits. I've climbed the tallest pine with Skip
Wiley trying to save an eagle, and played "The
Rain Guitar" on a bridge in Winchester.
I sat moodily in the sun on the Outer Banks after
finishing pirated rum, feeling the "Winds of the
Carolinas." I felt love make my soul crawl out of
its hiding place, with Zora...

I've sweat through Shelby Strother's Florida
summers when the air and the heat are the
same, and dreamt of dogs and endless walks in
the wilds of the Upper Peninsula of Michigan.
One day, giving a loose to my soul, I spent
chopping wood with Robert Frost.

Like Petty, I wouldn't back down and I met a
girl with a heart so big she could crush this
town. I've stood on a ledge and prayed to the
Maker of Life for Chingachgook, "The Last of
the Mohicans."

I've found my faith interwoven with doubt, and
allowed the flight of a single bird to dismiss my
turmoil. I've sat by myself in a "Clean Well-
lighted Place," and lived with the inescapable
full measure of loneliness.

I've watched thousands of sunsets, each with a
dose of Conroy's words. I've gone to the woods
to live deliberately and sailed "Into the Mystic."
I've worn Springsteen's "Brilliant Disguise" in a
flannel shirt, and I followed "The Songlines"
with Bruce Chatwin.

I had an interstate running through my front
yard and thought I had it so good, and I've
heard the white porpoise singing in the river of
time with a thousand dolphins in radiant
attendance. I've burned the candle at both ends
with St. Vincent Millay. I was a "Secondhand
Lion," believing in things that weren't
necessarily true but worth believing in...
all because, like Conroy, "I listened to my
English teachers," and to my friends and
mentors, and I too soaked up what those
magnificent men and women had to give. And I
also cherish and praise them and thank them for
finding me and presenting me with the precious
gift of the English language.

Love and Freedom

We just got back last night
From Western Carolina,
A quick trip up to the mountains, again
Then back down 26 to 95.
For me, an eleven-hour drive,
My son can make it in ten.

There, outside a little town called Leicester —
Up there it rhymes with Chester,
As in "Wait a minute Chester,
I'm a peaceful man."
Anyway, the family has a piece of land
Where I can go
Into the woods and pretend to be Thoreau.

And if I can, discover, or rediscover
My glorious pre-existing condition,
Free agency by definition,
Is life without hindrance or restraints,
Allowing me to see
Just what the picture paints.

Walking in the woods behind the dog
Above the cabin,
Up the mountain path
Winding through the oak and the hickory
And the sourwood trees,
Doing just what I want,
Thinking what I damn well please.

Going my own way —
Independent,
And free from what the neighbors say.
No roles or types
Cast in my direction.
Oh, I'm hoping that I like the guy that I see now
In the shallow creek's reflection.

Squinting upward through the branches
At the pale blue sky,
The chance to reflect
Strips me clean of any alibi.
Free agency, I suspect,
Is a beginning and not an end —
A cause and not just some effect…
Freedom is more than that, my friend.

I would have stayed longer
In my beloved Appalachians,
But that's all the time we had to spend.
Soon, no doubt I'll be headed up again.
Headed up or headed out offshore
"How does it feel?" asked Dylan —
To be on my own — just free willin'?
To be left alone?
Pretty damn good, actually.

But if this was about freedom,
I had to come back.
Like HDT, my trip was no retreat,
And the all-important act,
The necessary feat
Was the fact that I returned from isolation,
Bringing with me
Some truth about emancipation.
To be really free,
I had to shake off self-possession
And reconcile my habitation.

Now, a part of me would just as soon
Be out of tune
With the rest of the world,
And that's alright. That's okay,
But in living as a hermit, you just might find
The solitary life makes choices for you.

But once upon returning to a place
Shared knowingly with other folk —
Within sight of someone else's chimney smoke,
I must willfully concede
Limits to my independence.
As did my ancestors,
And so, it goes with me and my descendants.

As a member of the human race,
I must decide to act in such a way
Relevant to anyone
With whom I share a space.

My right to blast the Allman Brothers
Ends with the rights and precious ears of others.
Oh, but everybody loves the Allmans,
Look around! Can anyone say in good faith,
"Turn it down?"
But there's somebody out there, you know,
Who's never heard of *Eat a Peach,*
And this American thing
Is all about the rights of each.
Not just some of us, or most of us.
But all of us.

Never mind this writer
And the folly of his sins.
Holmes the Justice, not the fighter
Said your right to swing your fist
Ends where my old nose begins.

If we can't see with our own eyes,
If we don't recognize
The true meaning of the flag we fly —
What freedom really is,
We just may let it slip on by.

Here, back at home, I'm sure
Had I not taken steps to rein it in,
I may well have lost her.
Beware, for License is Liberty's imposter.

A free life, for better or for worse,
Oftentimes requires putting others first.
But how? Long I stood on that old mountain,
Believing reciprocity is all we needed.
You know, treat folks the way
You wish to be so treated.
And the one I hold most dear,
Of all of Lincoln's lessons that I save,
Is how he taught me that I cannot be a master
If I will not be a slave.

But isn't the giving of yourself
The purest meaning of love?
And so, then it is the drive, the push, the shove
Towards freedom?
I guess that's what I'm trying to say.
 It's not so complicated. We do it for our loved ones
Each and every day.
We take it as easy as the opening of a door
For it is the great liberating act of loving more.

And what is love? Well, I think I know.
Surely, it's an overflow
Of passion and emotion.
An electric touch.
But it's not just a falling of head over heels.
Love is a commitment to causes,
A dedication to ideals.

Inside us flows a natural spring,
Fed by the giving of oneself
To someone
Or to a certain thing.

Love, said Auden, is about paying attention.
How about that?
It's the nurturing of friendships and kinships
And the modesty of intention.

Great sacrifice,
And the satisfaction that comes
With that which we give up,
Fills and spills our blessing cup.
And it all comes down to this.

Now, every once in a while,
We need to go back to the woods, so to speak,
And remember what it's about.
Soon enough, no doubt,
I'll be headed up or headed out.
Maybe I'll just take a walk along the beach
And spend a sliver of time
Beyond the social reach.
Listen to my inner voice,
And get all reacquainted
With my free will and choice,
And what it had to teach.

Even fleeting moments
Without hindrance or restraints,
Can allow me to see just what the picture paints:

Beyond self-reliance and beyond free agency,
Lies liberty.
And it seems to me
That there in love's pursuit and nowhere else,
We are set free.

Floridian

I first saw him standing there
In Melbourne High School's freezing gym,
Witnessing the winning shot
Bouncing off the rim.

The tail of a red Hawaiian shirt
Hung out from beneath his flannel,
Serving as a coat.
He chatted with the passerby,
 Jotting down a random note.

That first image makes me smile,
I can still close my eyes and see him —
A Floridian — Florida boy, all the while.
 …all the while.

He loved Eastern Central Florida
But his talents took him far and wide.
North and West across the Continent's Divide.
From Denver to Detroit,
His stories filled an empty space,
But he could not hide his sense of place.
No matter where he went,
How far he was away,
Each and every day
He wore those tropic prints
Before and happily ever since.

Some were gaudy. Some were loud,
Right out of Jimmy's concert crowd.
A few were frayed around the collar
And the sleeves,
Perhaps there is a hint of what the man believes,
Floridian wore them proud.
But don't judge a book by its shirt.

I thought a lot of that guy —
Never told him though.
Figured he was sharp enough to know
But that's alright. That's okay.
If I had to do it all again,
I know exactly what I'd say.
His memory is safe with me.
It won't grow dim,
I'll pass along his stories
And wear these shirts each day
As a way to honor him.

"Still so much to be done," the old sailor sings.
Of the joy and pain that living brings.
But I think he had it figured,
Maybe from the start.
It's the dozens of little things
That make a life a work of art.

We may be blinded to the goings-on
By blazing sun and stinging rains.
And it's so hard at times
To see the love and beauty
In the relics and remains.

Oh, how time races along,
But there are Things that capture time
And keep it still…briefly.
As still as a Florida summer morning.

While on this Earth
He wrote a lot
About what he saw and heard
And what he thought.
Each link in chain, he worked the words,
Between the perfect and the almost perfect —
There is a difference, you know.

He got it down on paper — transitory moments
And mysteries revealed,
Of fleeting commonplace events
On boats and courts and playing fields.

There was always something.
About baseball and basketball
And knocking down the Berlin Wall.
  ...of Dad and Mom and Vietnam.
A painted dusk and blazing dawn
And stories of old Honest John.
Ever read that one?

Biographs and Epitaphs,
A Cracker Woman who shook all over
When she laughed.
...when she laughed.

So again, in answering your question,
I wear the shirts
As often as I can
To remember — to remind me of a man
With soul —
What the jazzman said makes other folks
Feel better about being alive.

Biograph Update
(So far)

He dove down into the clear green water of the
Atlantic; he read the Declaration of
Independence…studied it; made fires in all
kinds of weather; dodged a waterspout in the
Gulf… jumped off a railroad bridge into the
Peace River;   drank Mexican beer. He played
centerfield; fell off a roof, had a job digging
ditches. Sang songs to his children as they fell
asleep; burned some bridges; slid down a North
Carolina rock into freezing water; broke some
rules…stumbled while watching a beautiful girl
pass by…smoked a Cuban cigar. Ruined
friendships over pride…saved some friendships
by swallowing his pride.

Got born and raised in Florida…Melbourne,
Florida, that is. He saw dolphins jump not
twenty feet from the bow of his boat…he read
the Bill of Rights as often as he could; kept some
secrets; sometimes played his music too loud.

He once cursed and prayed in the same
sentence. He loved books…liked the way books
smelled — old and new…wrote a book…loved
baseball. He got seasick occasionally; nearly
broke his ankle jumping into shallow water near
Shell Island. Played catch with his son; he
passed down stories of the great Ted Williams;
got his ego in the way; tried to listen to advice,
didn't always follow it. Felt guilty, at times for
good reason— other times, for no good reason.

He pretended not to see someone he knew… got
his feelings hurt when someone he knew
pretended not to see him. Loved his wife and
kids and dogs. Dove down into the coke bottle
green water of the Gulf of Mexico; stayed awake
all night; read Robert Frost to his children.

Fell asleep at the wheel. Got upset at a priest for his homily…changed his mind because of priest's homily. He took walks alone on the beach…went to Monticello; sat upon a surfboard out beyond the break and listened to the silence…read his favorite books over and over again…spent a lot of time in the Keys…went to a John Mellencamp concert; piloted his boat through a driving rain storm; got speeding tickets while listening to John Mellencamp and Tom Petty. Defended Marilyn Monroe's honor; he felt the hair stand up on the back of his neck during The Star-Spangled Banner.

Saw Roberto Clemente play baseball…cultivated his Irish; took family walks along the beach…loved his English teachers. He held his granddaughters, Savannah, Delaney, and Amelia.

…was known on occasion to scream at the television while watching political speeches; told the same stories over and over again, even when he was younger. He helped a few people…missed a lot of opportunities to help others. Read Zora Neale Hurston…watched the sunrise on the Sebastian Inlet jetty…took a swim in Brick Lake. He was by his father's side when he died…

He stood his ground when he should have given in; drank coffee from Café du Monde; tossed a quarter in the fish's mouth at Captain Tony's…he once met Captain Tony…had his picture taken with Captain Tony. Stopped going to Church after his mother died. Saw Pete Rose and George Brett play baseball; climbed a waterfall in Jamaica; he loved dogs…did I tell you he loved dogs? He read newspaper columns by Billy Cox; smoked a few cheap cigars.

He went back to Church after his kids were
born. Talked to neighbors; slept in a hammock
one summer; avoided neighbors. Gave in when
he should have stood his ground; cussed when
he was angry…threw things when he was very
angry, once bought a six-pack of beer with
change. He loved the city of Savannah…pirated
cobblestones from River Street in Savannah…
Saw Carl Yastremski play left field...

Ran out of gas; read Thomas Paine's "Common
Sense" several times; avoided phone-calls;
picked up trash out of the river; watched "The
Quiet Man" each and every St. Patrick's Day.
Argued with umpires; talked to God; saw Willie
Mays play baseball; loved the Pittsburgh
Steelers. Steered his boat through 8-foot swells
and wondered if he would see land again…
talked too much…drank too much…didn't talk
enough…at times, didn't drink enough.

Tried to make eye contact as much as possible;
cried at his daughter's dance recital… he spent
numerous evenings waiting for a full moon to
rise up out of the ocean…took his kids fishing;
defended JFK's honor… gauged a man by his
handshake.

…sat in the dark listening to Van Morrison; ate
guava pie; studied the US Constitution; ripped
the buttons off his shirt the night the Braves beat
the Pirates for the pennant. Drank Guinness at
Kevin Barry's in Savannah…let his dogs run on
the beach—Melbourne Beach, St. George,
Hatteras…

He had his boat break down right in the middle
of Sebastian Inlet...He read Jim Harrison; loved
kids; quoted Thomas Jefferson and Bob Dylan in
the same conversation — had a grandson named
Dylan. He tried to have a firm handshake;
bought his daughter a steel drum; got tears in
his eyes the first time his son rode a bicycle.
Took a 6-hour boat ride to Cabbage Key; ate
fresh snapper fried light; once chopped down a
tree onto the power lines; sat in the driving rain
at a Florida-Georgia football game...liked to sit
with friends around a bonfire.

...he talked often to his mother; listened to John
Prine for half a century...admired Eugene V.
Debs. Once went to Charleston, South Carolina
by accident; wore tropical shirts as often as he
could; he quoted his father daily. Hit a grand
slam, built a Tiki bar, walked through
graveyards in Connecticut, hitched a ride on a
boat to get pizza. Read Louis L'Amour's
"Mangrove Coast"...admired Martin Luther
King, Jr...admired Robert E. Lee and Alice Paul.
He once had a job teaching history.

...read James Dickey's "Rain Guitar" a hundred
times but never memorized it; had a tire swing;
made strange mobiles out of shells, driftwood,
and crabtrap floats. He once had a job moving
furniture; wrote letters to the editor of the local
newspaper but seldom got them printed...had a
Christmas in July party...once had two German
Shepherds; drove a Jeep Wagoneer to the top of
a mountain; walked through a graveyard in
Apalachicola...played a ballgame while the
KKK sat out beyond
the left field fence.

Twice stood on the steps of the Lincoln
Memorial — once with his kids...listened to
Waylon Jennings...and Willie Nelson...and Kris
Kristofferson...and Merle Haggard...and
Johnny Cash. He prayed while driving; fell for
his wife on the Fourth of July.

He voted for Clinton Tyree for governor; saw
just about every movie Robert Duvall ever
made; read Carl Sandburg; built a swing off of
the side of a North Carolina mountain...sang
songs to his wife and kids (while they rolled
their eyes). He liked to sit by himself around a
bonfire.
Coached high school baseball; listened a lot to
Bruce Springsteen... owned a 1985 23-foot
Mako. He liked to watch the phosphorescence
in the wake of a boat; was thrown out of a bar;
wore out several baseball caps — wore them
out...lost touch with good friends...let his son
drive...he watched "Donovan's Reef" each
Christmas. He knew how to hook slide;
collected license plates; had a Chocolate Lab
named Marley — before the book and movie, but
after the prophet. He loved the Florida
Gators...loved to cook chicken on the grill.

...got lost quite a few times but rarely admitted
it; mooned a cruise ship; found spiritual
meaning in Jimmy Buffett songs; quoted
Abraham Lincoln daily; kept people at arm's
length so he could see them better; read
"Siddhartha"...wrote poems to his wife...loved
listening to BB King, Albert King, Stevie Ray
Vaughn, and Carlos Santana play
guitar...quoted Nelson Mandela; watched Field
of Dreams; named his son after his great
grandfathers and George Brett; went sledding
down an icy mountain road; smoked his father's
pipe; cried when John Prine died.

He read John Steinbeck's biography of Captain Henry Morgan…loved to laugh at Chris Farley and John Belushi and Will Farrell…had a few real good friends; read two Hemingway biographies…loved beer; learned to like red wine; listened to strangers…got the blues…played the blues to get rid of them.

He read just about everything Carl Hiaasen's written, stopped going to Disneyworld after reading Hiaasen…built a deck; built several decks; built a porch with a tin roof…He carved his name on a channel marker by a mangrove island called Jackass Key. He liked to be by himself; listened to what Bob Marley had to say; water--skied behind a pickup truck…
…had a yellow dog named Summer—a great dog, great friend…and a refugee Lab called Indie, with dark dark eyes—another good friend. He played the Allman Brothers loud and often.

He got grumpy; grew a beard; saw sea turtles offshore…bragged about his kids; took his dogs by boat to the spoils islands in the intracoastal… wrote a children's book about dogs, and befriended a feral cat. He cried when the Steelers won the Super Bowl…had hurricane parties; bought a 1973 Ford Bronco…listened to what John Wayne had to say. Lost a grandson.

…wore two-dollar flip-flops…spent most of his life wearing flip-flops; he wore cowboy boots for a while then went back to flip flops; coached college baseball; named a boat "Plan B"…loved the Dave Matthews Band; had a Belgian Shepherd named Stella Grace. He once skipped work and went to Mass, skipped Mass and went to the beach, several times…had fist-fights, and lost…wrote poetry…once owned an old Jeep…

took his kids out of school to go boating…he's
been to Amelia Island, Pelican Island, Tybee
Island, Merritt Island, Roanoke Island, Egmont
Key, Little Torch Key, and Gainesville…and as
James Taylor said, he always thought he'd see
you again…

The Gift I Never Gave

Of all the gifts I never gave
To say to you, one day,
You are my sister chosen,
There is one that haunts me
For the way I let it slip away.

There were three birch logs
A neighbor kept for decoration.
It seemed to me it was beyond her ken —
The worth of wood and depth of adoration.

She could not comprehend the value
Nor understand the cost
For the gift your father gave us.
Reading Robert Frost.

When she moved on,
I wanted little
Of her selling and her giving
As she was cleaning out,
Ridding fifty years of living.
Still, she promised me the birches…
But she forgot somehow
In all her hurried pace
And the birch logs disappeared.
Gone without a trace.
Having those upon your hearth,

It would be truly grand Harkening tradition.
But here I stand with empty hands
Mired in contrition.

For both the reader and writer Verse cuts deep
beneath the skin; It can bring us closer to our Maker
Or wake the pagan ghost within. And so, we grasp
for things
That conjure up the golden moments
As we race along —
Reminding us of treasures
In books and poems and song.

Of all the gifts I never gave to say to you
The things I should,
It is this verse I send
On lost but not forgotten wood.

For may it remind you
Of swingers of birches.
That poetry is truth
And forests are churches.

Shade

A timeless sun bears down on ancient trees.
The shade is new again today
And I am held at bay
To feel the breath of breeze.
To sit beneath and sip my drink
And think
 Of everything… or nothing.
I look up sometimes
And squint,
To make the trees something of Monet`.
Shards of light between the leaves
Give hint to what this fool perceives —
That he has gotten something different
From this day.
 Shade. Perhaps
A thing between what Frost would call
 "The local green and universal blue."
Can this be true?
I just know of shade beneath
The palms and oaks.
Or underneath the bridges
Sought by wayward souls and homeless folks
And the sigh of satisfaction
From my brown dog
Upon finding it under…anything.
Once two hurricanes struck back-to-back
And tore my trees to smithereens,
Leaving me languishing
In a humid Florida September.
I sat miserable in the sun.
And the oaks said, "we're tired,
Find another place, will you."
The leaning palms pleaded,
"Give us a break from your ponderings."
But still I sat
Hopeful,
When I could, waiting for the shade to return.
And it did.

Boatman's Lament

Highway out your window
Traffic in your ear.
Can't pretend that it's the ocean anymore.

She's been gone now several hours —
Feels like a friggin' year,
Like she got right up
And walked out of your door.
She was your prized possession,
Now you're stuck here in the sand.
Magnificent obsession —
And no one but your brother understands.

Play that record on the stereo —
Side B "A1A"
Drink yourself into a stupor,
You sold your boat today.

Starboard listing toward your right mind
But never known for common sense.
When the world closed in around you,
She was your last defense.

A boatman's occupation,
Folks think you're half insane,
Now this captive habitation
Seems borderline profane!
Sunset in your pocket
Saltwater on the brain.
A breeze across the porch today
Cannot begin to ease the pain.

Old record on the stereo — side B "A1A"
Play the music louder.
You sold your boat today.

Late Frost

In dim lamplight I did recline,
Pondering an old Frost line
While sipping my tea
There beneath an old,
Yellowed nautical map of Savannah.

And the words they harkened back
To many evenings past —
When I was all caught up
In the romance of defiance
And things not meant to last.

I remembered being troubled
By his observation,
When once I read his words
With youthful indignation.
All that I could hear inside that rock hard head
Was the politician's righteous call
For tearing down
And not the mending of a wall.

Words would surely rise — poetic inspiration —
Bearing witness to the moment
Of its disintegration.
He would have been compelled to tell
Of how he felt the freedom when it fell.

The precious paperback
Was secondhand I bought
But the sense behind
This verse I thought
Was mine and only mine.
Surely others claimed this too,
With the best of all intention.
For we could only see the world
In a single stark dimension.
But I had hunted down the metaphor and killed it.

But older now,
Lamenting my back pages
And paying age's wages
In times of change beyond our ken,
I take refuge in my modest den.

Remember Hemingway,
Who liked to say, Perhaps
We grow not wiser, just more careful.
The poet's walls and trees
Aren't just walls and trees.
And his neighbor surely occupied
More than acres in the countryside.
But who am I to say?

So,
In bright sunlight,
I do resign
To build the walls
And walk the line.
I mix the mud,
I lay the block eight courses high.
I set the posts down deep.
I run the wire,
I nail the boards.
What does this signify?
But a promise that I keep.
In fighting off the modern world
It's a promise to myself
As I place a tattered copy
Of his collected works back upon the shelf.

A Brush With Life

First time on the boat in months,
Just a little peace they hoped to find
But there was paperwork and deadlines
And Monday on her mind.

With a sigh of Sunday evening
As they moved on through the bay,
Breaking clean the human silence,
She said, *we can't go on this way.*

There's something about this working life
That seems so damn profane.
Rolling rocks from place to place
And man, it's driving me insane!

The world is too much with me
I know the poet said,
And I am lost somewhere between
My yearning and my dread.

For the getting and the spending
We give ourselves away –
My time is slipping through my fingers
Day by day by day.

Take me out, take me back, take me away!
Let's chase the sun as far as we can go.
Take me out, lay me down, love me away,
The way you did so many years ago.
Heat it up, boil it down, boil it over!
Out into the Gulf of Mexico...

So, he took her to a holy place
Beyond the sight of land
And there beneath a painted sky,
She came again to understand.

He said, *In that coat and tie*
I fear I am a dead man,
But I had a brush with life one time out here.
Just trolling for the closure of a sunset--
Playing Caribbean music sipping beer.

You know, we rage against the selling out
And pay the daily toll.
We pull our weight and tow the line
For moments we feel whole.

And I have found religion here
In the colors of the early morn,
Like I saw it in your eyes
The days our kids were born.

This is why I work –
What living is to me!
Then he took her by the hand
And watched the sun fall in the sea.

There was no room inside a church for this
So, they cast their guilt aside,
Then promised to each other
To live this life until they died

One True Line

On a day that was stolen
From the seeds I have sown —
With some time that was borrowed,
On a boat I half own.
Beneath a sky that was given
In a mood that I found,
I tried to write one true line
From a heart that is mine.

Equilibrium

I got up early Thursday and slipped out quietly
So not to wake my wife and son and daughter.
I drove across the causeway
To celebrate my birthday
Watching the sun rise out of the water.
It had spent the last three months boiling the
Atlantic: A hurricane was brewing
Five hundred miles from here.
Still, I observed my pagan ritual
For the passing of a year:
With a thermos and a cooler —
Hot coffee and cold beer.

Last Chance at First Light

Last chance at first light —
There's a vow I must keep,
Can't fall back asleep.
I've got to get down
To the boat ramps right now.
I promised my kids; I promised myself
That this day would break over the bow…

One Day Came

Known just by number
Not by name,
One day, now broken.
One day dawned…one day came down
But somehow not here and gone —
It keeps hanging 'round.
Time has dulled the edges —
And tempered by the fire, we pretend to heal.
Again, we chase our hungers and desires —

Ain't that America, says the Indiana man —
But as we try to understand, as we sit and fret,
I can't help but think that we lament the loss
Of something deeper yet.

And like an old river,
We take the path of least resistance,
All the while not knowing where it leads.
Cutting through the clay,
Meandering through the grass and reeds.
On this wayless way,
We satisfy the mortal needs.
But all the getting and the spending
Cannot keep us safe and warm
And write the happy ending.

There is a gulf between us and our creed
That sends one back to bookshelves,
Searching for a wisdom we can heed.
The New Englander is there to say
What it is exactly
He thinks is missing on this day —

It is ourselves that we withhold
Which dims the light.
We must give the gift outright…

Now, Lincoln said it best —
Just pass the Declaration's test:
Believe that crazy proposition
That we're born free and equal,
And you walk with Jefferson.

But there's three hundred million of us!
We spend our days, apart —
Attending to our habits of the heart.
Going our separate ways,
Denying all along every instinct of the herd.

I've got my music--you've got yours
And they tell me we are tied
By some belief that only living free can bring?
The proverb says it's not the song,
But in the fact, we sing!

That deed of gift, said Frost, is war, however,
And as one day broken
Changed us all forever more,
Will it come together
The way it's never been before?
It may be the story has only just begun.

As in the ancient allegory,
Our eyes adjusted to the sun,
Only now can see what's real,
Though some return to caves,
Preferring shadows on the wall
Confused and overwhelmed by the fury of it all,
Others find catharsis in the fire…
And once again,
The hymn may well have found a choir.
Will this ordeal; this test
Prove the creed is stronger than the steel?

One day dawned…one day came down
But somehow not here and gone —
It keeps hanging 'round.

To the Ticking Clock

Where he once could not abide
To chronicle the time or tide,
He's taken now to wear a watch
On quiet walks downtown.
Is it innocence revisited?
Wisdom lost or found?
He's given now to sip his scotch
Where once he gulped it down.

And to keep his mind unbound —
To see the beauty all around.
He now lifts his head up from the grind.
Paying close attention,
When once he paid no mind.

Now he flies away on daydreams,
Not shackled to the ground.
Where once he spread his life so thin,
Now, he boils it down.

Bio

Jim McGinnis is a native Floridian, still residing in his hometown of Melbourne after 63 years. He's a husband, father, grandfather, brother, uncle, teacher, coach, writer, and some say a dog-whisperer (rumor has it).

He is the author of three other books — *Tending to The Past, Points South,* and a children's book called *Good Dog Loose.*

The author has also published over 40 episodes on his podcast, "Stories We Can Tell (anchor.fm/jim-mcginnis), and he's posted many video readings of his work on Facebook and YouTube (@jimmcginnis-letterstobrown6994).

McGinnis spends much of his free time outdoors. He loves kids and dogs, oaks and palms, beaches and boats…and ballparks.

https://www.amazon.com/author/jim.mcginnis